Her Poetic Truth

A Journey Through Poetry

TARIKUA EMIRU

ISBN (hardcover): 978-1-7367729-0-4
ISBN (paperback): 978-1-7367729-1-1
ISBN (ebook): 978-1-7367729-2-8

Illustrations

Sideline: Atanur Memis, Pooch Studio (Model Adut Atem)

Pexels: Truth Enock; Bran Sodre; Jairo David Arboleda: Bestbe Modesl, Filipe Gomes; Bash Mutumba; Follow Alice

Editor: Nicole Fegan
Designer: Euan Monaghan

May my legacy be one you carry proudly; may my name be a name you say with distinction and clarity.

To my loves- Mickey and Nola, it was through your birth that I truly emerged. I pray my body of work leaves a legacy that you will carry with pride and joy. To my husband Kelelaye, I thank you for your trust in my vision, and your unwavering support and love.

To my big brother Henok, for sharing some of the best advice over the years, and having my back since birth, love you always.

To all my family and dear friends, who encouraged, loved, and spoke gifts of affirmations over me, I am eternally grateful.

To all those reading these words, I pray you never stop believing in your dreams, If you're able to see the vision, God has already made the provision.

May love, compassion, awakening and truth find you within these pages.

Thank you.

Forever in my heart, and always in my thoughts, I share this dream with you Mom

Table of Contents

GPS

I don't fit into this life that I've been cast in.
I tried to acclimate, but I've outgrown my past,
And the past is in my present with the future on my back, and
I'm spinning trying to find my footing with my hands behind my back.

I don't recognize my own reflection, and it's affecting my what-to-do's.
See, I'm drowning in this season while I quarantine and process
my next move.
It's nothing personal, nothing against any of you,
I just need some time and space to meditate and pray, for only
God can see me through.

Seeking validation over self-preservation, I expired.
I stay voiceless on deaf ears.
I make moves, I stay quiet.

Life is so complicated with belated realizations.
Led with insecurity, now my foundation shows signs that it's been
shaken.

Fear has taken over navigations.
Feeling claustrophobic in expectations.
Many walk in shoes that are mistaken.
But one must never conform to what they see,
because God permits vision
to the blind if they believe.

So, while darkness feels limiting, I take comfort in knowing this:
Although I feel lost in my surroundings
God's GPS will redirect.

Petals

Petals fell from me.......slowly.
As the wind brushed my hair, as the seasons changed, I tried to
hold onto the petals with my feet and my hands.
I tried to whisper, walked on my tip-toes, moved delicately, but
they still fell on the floor.
I stood still and let the wind hit me, tired of losing the battle daily.
I stood aware and unaware it was the struggle that left me bare.

When I stopped trying to hold onto the petals....
I let go of the fear, the voices in my head that said,
"For what is a flower without petals, my dear?"
I let the dead petals leave with no plea.
Echoed from my soul, "I release you of your responsibilities."
I began to slowly peer my eyes open , and I took a deep breath;
I was ready to see what was left.
To my delight and surprise, I had abundant petals growing and
was now bearing fruit.
When releasing what is dead, living takes root.

Lost

Yesterday, I found a piece of you; it was wrapped in a box labeled "Lost."
Upon opening the box, I found a note in a brown envelope with
no return address, and just this simple quote:
"Find me when you're ready to fly, when you've let go of your
inhibition, leaping beyond the clouds of judgment and criticism to
soar past the stars in the sky, leading with your heart and soul....
flying with me with no fear of the fall below."

I closed the lid and placed that box back in your attic of fear.

Inheritance

I pass down wisdom.
Etched into each strand,
I, with my hands, leave lessons as my inheritance.
From they to she to me to her,
I grasp the hands and lead so she can learn
that in her veins, she carries grace beyond circumstance.
Character is woven, strength married with resilience yet relegated
    to back rooms 'cause our presence hints at a power beyond their
    aptitude.
We observe and retain; our eyes capture the capacity to see
    through strategies.
They see women; we be the womb of man.
We birth what they can't understand.
Braided into each strand, I lay my inheritance.

Mogul

There is fire in my poetry,
Ancestors awake to what I'm saying.
As I dust off the former self to be the "she"
that rests in these pages.
Tell them I'm a mogul in these words I speak. Even nature takes
notice of the Matrix.

I light it up and watch the pages be
Her Poetic pages

Wings

Hey little girl, I remember you….
You were once filled with dreams bigger than a room.
Three bedrooms in your mom's flat, yet the bathroom was the one
    in which you felt safe to practice your craft.
You would climb the sink and stretch your arms real wide,
    pretending they were wings.
In the mirror, you'd be found rehearsing your lines, fostering your
    dreams, thanking the academy for recognizing a Queen.
You were going to fly past the glass ceilings far beyond sensibility,
    into a cloud of endless possibilities.
Spanning wide, capturing every firefly,
and as you walked across the stage, you would nod your head and
    wave,
feeling worthy and entitled to the awards and accolades….
Yea, I remember you….

When does the rapture eclipse the sun?
When do children's aspirations get nursed as grown-ups'
    inhibitions?
Why do we settle for average while we numb our souls' pleas for
    creativity and liberation, to live the lives we've always dreamed?

We now immortalize celebrities, spend hours tracking trends and
    feeds.
Live vicariously through fictitious realities, escaping the reality that
    each day is an opportunity to create our own legacies.
Tragedy: we patronize children for their curiosity, when their
    wonder and fire are what we aspire to.

We drown in self-help books, filter versions of our physical looks,

when internal struggle wages war, the child in us demanding
   more.
Adults control both a.m. and p.m. yet in between them is stillness.
Seconds that turned into minutes, and minutes into days, years
   that pass and still we're mentally enslaved.
Jaded in our ways, becoming untrusting, less loving, walking
   around in a bit of a haze, while it remains—

The little girl on the bathroom floor, climbing to the sink,
   stretching her arms as wings, waiting for you to believe that she
   can be anything she dreams.

She

She doesn't even know her strength, her ability to rise above the
adversities of this life that she was dealt.
She,
She has been kicked, choked, and knocked down at each turn, and
used her knuckles to pick up carry on, and learn.
She,
She walks with class and elegance, yet her personal life shows
evidence of extreme turbulence.
She,
She is your sister, your mother, your friend; gives you more of
herself than herself even can.
She,
She is up with you late at night, knees sore from praying, eyes sore
from crying, arms ready to fight.
She,
She is your sister, mother, wife, looked past, taken for granted,
disconnected from your life.

Bag Lady

This world is cold some ride the wave to feel some warmth in it.
While some close their eyes to shield their minds , too hard to
cope with it.
We walk around carrying trauma in both hands -like a bag lady;
Paralyzing our mobility to grow,
too afraid to deal so search for coping methods to numb the hole.
Some shake their ass to satisfy thirst of being seen .
Some drown their sorrow in bottles that are unclean .
While, some smoke to rise to an elevated state.
Baggage carried to different destinations
in a myriad of suitcases.

(She) Remix

She's the fly "Tender Roni" type.

Knees ready to pray and arms ready to fight.

The "Homie, Lover, Friend," live conversations, passionate
engagements, the type to give you herself, more than herself
even can.

She's the forever type of lady.

The one that sees past your maybes into your ambition, past the
circumference of your inhibitions to realize what you've been
missing.

The "Love Jones" type of Mrs.

The one that reads behind the label for the fine print, she's that
Unapologetic, Queen vibes type of chick.

Beauty Mark

I saw beauty once… and it looked so effortless.

I reached out my hands but my grasp couldn't manage it.

Then it spoke—

I looked around, bewildered that beauty as such could make a sound;

and the sound was directed at me; amazed, I thought, "well, how could this be?".

Reluctant, I drew near, trying to quiet the noise around me; poised, I lent my ears. Then it whispered…

but I couldn't make out the words, each line drawn was its own poetry verse.

I blinked and beauty disappeared, stood cemented and grateful to have encountered beauty so rare.

I would have thought it a dream had it not been for the reverberance in my heart.

That one night beauty left its mark.

Establishment

There is an establishment
Hidden away, woven into generations, tucked and stowed,
declaring unwaveringly that
WE are unable.
Unworthy.
Unwilling to accept our places deemed "suitable";
That, if perchance we do dare and move past a line, ominous
    things may occur.
But....
Dare we do—dream, be, leap using the line drawn not as the
    limit, but as the marker that will propel us into the endowment
    entrusted when created as a woman.

Black Hair

Let me tell you about the hands that lay hands on my hair.
As I sit between the legs that sat between theirs.
It's a rich tradition-
roots married with posture
styles signifying our culture;
From expressive to subdued,
natural to infused,
in simpatico with our hair is our attitude.
We choose
who we are and who we're not.
From curls to faux locks,
bantu twists to crimps
speaking language you don't think exists.

We have
quite an agency to translate and express our:
versatility
ingenuity
creativity;
and we be- fly while doing so.
From bald fades, to locs,
afros and wash and go's,
colors in every fold.

We know
our dexterity is admired.
We hold,
secrets many wish to aspire.
We show,
how protective we are of our roots; by teach our young ones how
to cultivate, foster, and produce.

Whether wrapped in a scarf or displayed in bold
our kinswomen winning all across the globe.
Multilingual is hair our hair we know
garners stares and critiques-
some use bifocals to examine and uncover our mystique.
When unable to imitate barriers set up to promote normalcy
But that's not who we be; we dismiss normalcy with faux pas
hostility.

Our hair is revolutionary on its own.
It can make statements without uttering a tone.
Many try to touch to decipher the code,
no mystery here, those that know- know,
Our crown is a passed-down legacy an inheritance we unfold.

We rock and celebrate our hair identity.
From locs, to senegalese twists, curls, box braids—micro and
knotless—
afros in all forms, natural or pressed down,
mohawks, finger waves, or in dreads now;

We salute sisters with a bow, unwritten language we acknowledge
with a smile.

Mama Africa

I departed from you at such a young age; like a distant relative to me you became.
On TV, they represented you as weak and showed babies, malnourished with overgrown bellies.
They showed dirt roads, captured rural terrain; children swarmed with bees seeming rather unfazed.
The children carried beautiful smiles but eyes that had matured past their age.

I too was a child and watched it all with empathy and disdain.

At home, Mom would contrast the images by telling me how beautiful you were, and how delish the dishes, how authentic and different; the contrasting views left me feeling indifferent.

I went to school without many others that looked like you, so, like a secret, I hid who you were from the rest of the room.

International Day came, where our native mothers had to be on display. Ignorance filled the room like a tidal wave. "Friends" at school, curious and unaware, asked, "Does your mother feed you, do you guys even eat? I saw your people last night on the TV."

With tears, I ran home with weak knees. Anger and shame stirred within me.

Mom grabbed me by the hand and put my head on her knees. She stroked my hair and sang, recounting your beauty.

When I told her what they said, she chuckled and shook her head, saying,

"Ayeee! Nothing is like back home, my dear; don't eat the lack of knowledge that they spit out of fear. The blood in our veins comes from history that's been painful, but still, we sustained. Poor? …..Hmm."

She carried on:

"Like a rich man who's been robbed, we've been stripped, with our eyes open but our hands bound. Third world, yes, but the soil is so rich, we are blessed with natural resources, coca, berries, coffee beans." She then started telling me of her childhood memories.

"Poor?" she came back to say:

"Rich is our history and culture, rich are we in our traditions, rich we are, formed to pay respect to our elders. Rich in our beauty that's been emulated in media you see; our curves are a natural part of our anatomy. The media would rather call a drawing beautiful than the reality." That was long ago; that lesson carried the essence of my pride of "back home."

Bore an emperor and empress, and your name was blessed on their lips. My son bore the beat of your drum, my daughter your strong spirit; they don't hide you like I once did. When someone asks them, "Where are you from?" They loudly proclaim, "Child of Mama Africa!

AFRICA

Captured with endless possibilities.
Land so rich it bore Kings and Queens.
Divided by ignorance and greed.
Seduced and gang-raped by foreign countries.
Stripped of jewels and our greatest commodities.
Endured generations of genocide, slavery and poverty.
Rawness in beauty, the abundance is its strength.
Freedom is a state of mind that we fight to protect.

Ethiopia

With pride and joy, I claim the land of the pure.

Colonizers tried, but they couldn't colonize an indigenous tribe.

Our dust is the sum of our ancestors.

In riches or in poverty, Ethiopia sovereign, not just a country but a
biblical prophecy.

Respect is bigger than currency, where serving one is equivalent to
serving many.

I'm proud of my identity.

My lineage is royalty.

Real Kings and Queens* recognize when to curtsy.

They brought armies with weapons, and we still defeated them, so
ask me the lesson….

The heart is bigger than the fist.

A group unified in love can resist like David conquering Goliath.

*Referencing Queen Elizabeth and Prince Phillip bowing before
Emperor Haile Selassie of Ethiopia and his wife Empress Menen
Asfew

VOICE

Stronger than the biggest tree.
Wiser now, my eyes can see your fight, your voice; your words are
written on my back;
I will carry you on my generations, generations, generations—
Tax.
I hear you whisper when I lie still,
I pray I can carry out your will,
I pray I can lead men and women alike, that I may stride in my
step and fight the uphill fight.
I will not stutter, nor will I back down; I will not cry for the tears
have been shed throughout.
I will not howl, no need to look away—I will stare them in the
eyes and say—
No more to your pity,
No more am I on my knees,
No more will I take you intruding your arrogance on me.
I am who I am, and who I am is me, no more apologies.
Enough of your history. You will learn my own.
Enough of you telling me what I can't control,
I am who I am, and who I am is ME, no more apologies.
What you hear now has been my voice within.
I must speak now for our children fate is in, not in your hands, or
the hands that have been.
I must breathe life to a life for life to begin.
These mediums are not a testament to the steps they have walked,
These images are not a testament to how hard they fought.
For you and I to be here has been a long walk.
I must speak now so our troubles don't get lost.
Open your eyes and look at me; I'm not what you've tried to make
me out to be.
Open your eyes and look at me, for I will not leave, and tomorrow

will still be ME.
Hear my voice as I speak, and the incline in my tone....

No more to your pity,
No more am I on my knees,
No more will I take you intruding your arrogance on me.
I am who I am, and who I am is me, no more apologies.
Enough of your history—you will learn my own.
Enough of you telling me what I can't control.
I am who I am and who I am is ME, no more apologies.

Ancestor

How do you begin to thank someone you don't know,
But know that without their existence, there wouldn't be as much growth?
How do you tell a soul that passed how much you feel blessed, for your tomorrow is shaped by their past?
Their stories engraved in our hearts; their tears embedded in our thoughts.

Their determination to sit when forced to stand.
Their unwillingness to hide their pride and to smile while some spat.
Ability to hold their head high, when taught at infancy to look down.
Their faith in knowing "this shall pass" was prophetic to carry them leaps and bounds.

Their days of imprisonment were for us to be free; thank you is merely not enough, is what I see.

Thank you doesn't repay or make way for more changes.
If we do not carry the torch, the next generation will be indebted and aimless.
How do we begin to thank our Ancestors?
Paying it forward, not turning our backs, standing in where we witness any gaps.
We honor and pay homage by remembering and telling their stories, being mindful in our teachings ,while celebrating their glories.

Chess

What's redemptive of a law that was conceptualized with a flaw?
Sectioning off truths and history while redlining misery.
How does one play chess with life, playing both King and Knight
    on an uneven corrupt plight, board set up and framed before
    men could even fight?

Where is the humanity in treating the sane with insanity?
Defecating on the liberty of a segmented group,
synthesizing portions of truth,
demonstrating ill powers of use.

Walking past injustice is tainting the sight of righteousness.
Poverty of mind is rampant when one can oblige that such breach
    of moral conduct doesn't affect lives.
Bleeding devasting repercussions on legacies.
Altering trajectories, breeding inequities.
Fanning the flames of disparity does not reduce the heat,
One must do more than speak.
Rally the bishops of the court.
Protect the Queen; she'll endure strength far greater than all the
    players on the team.
Study the laws; be comfortable in unfairness but strategic when
    faced with arrogance.
Checkmate is conceived when enlightenment is achieved.

Our relations (U.S)

I've tried to numb emotions with suppressed tokens.

Deflecting has always been my mode of coping.

Cascade falls enveloping while I'm frozen.

Rhetorical "I love yous"—years dissipating, musical chairs,
    sat in anticipation, but our relations fell last on your list of
    reparations.

Cumulative offense has grown into frustration.

Satirical, I would call my reservations;

believing in justice that's clearly vacant.

Cornrows

One strand, two strands, three strands no more.
Cornfield of rows; let's delve in and explore:

Cargo ships:
There are some standing,
some laying hip to hip,
aroma of fear, confusion, despair…

Hunger pangs
Twelve hours, 24 hours, lost the count of days.

What is this language that they speak?
Why such vile hate in their eyes and tone of speech?

Women stripped bare, children crying, *no longer crying.*
No tears, dried up droplets of fears.

My throat hoarse, no one in my village to assimilate. Foreign is
each related face.

Hands behind our bodies, ropes cutting off circulation, wrists
bleeding, twisted in frustration.

This ship, these waters, these men without borders. I choke on
helplessness, anger, confusion: what is this?
I do not understand what crime I have outstanding;
What sin did I commit?
What reparations can equate to such pernicious violations…
No language to articulate my growing frustrations.

I try to breathe; I lose my breath, loosen my hands. What is left?
The unknown, or my own demise—do I jump off this ship or
    stand rotting and die?

Black Man

Black man, black man, what do you see?

I see a whole nation plotting and conspiring against me.
I see urban planning not being challenged in our communities.
I see a justice system that's turned a blind eye, choking the
innocent, asserting its arrogance.
Media franchises buying ad time to display my kind in the worst light.
I see them telling us not to fight; in time, things will be right.
Generations later and black lives still don't matter, and yet it
matters, won't turn my eyes, time to confront the demons where
they lie.
Black man, black man, what do you hear ?

I hear a lot of abuse, misuse of my name with misconstrued truths.
My name synonymous with recklessness.
Black man is "an uneducated buffoon, criminal up to no good, a
thug, a liar a cheat and a thief. Born a bastard, raised by a single
mother grew to be an absent father."
All these lies told about me—lies sold as truths.
Sure, the stacks were dealt high against me, but perseverance is in
my roots. I am not the sum of my reality, although they wish I was;
I rise in spite of their abuse.
Black man, black man, what do you want to do?

Bear arms, not with our hands, bear arms with our minds;
Combat with Ta-Nehisi Coates, Malcolm X insights, Martin
Luther King notes.
James Baldwin's eloquent tongue, Nelson Mandela's resilience, for
modeling rectitude annihilate ignorance. Follow the teachings
of Dr. Sebi—health consciousness creates healthy tendencies, no
more being fed on GMO's, eating clean, keeping the vessel lean.

Spiritual strength cannot be neglected. Pray and fast, study the
word, for spiritual strength prepares for mental defeats.
Be what they fear most, a black man unwilling to play ghost.
Black man, black man, what do you need?

I need the support of my Queens. I need my brothers and sisters to
pick up their talents using their presence;
Rappers spit on growth and elevation; if you're a blogger, write on
gentrification.
Anything to spark positive awareness and conversation.
Take time to talk with the youth, pray for their homes, and be the
example of truth.
Sit in on city council meetings, elect representatives that unify and
uplift our communities. Challenge the boards of education; it's
about time we start developing textbooks with facts
rather than contradiction and fabrications.
No more false narratives. Time to teach our kids the real history
the facts on their heritage.

Black man, black man, who are you?

I am the hero and the villain, the truth to the misconceptions, the
strength and dream of my ancestors; I am history, I am present, I
am the future.

Colored Girl

I'm taking back the term a "colored girl"... 'cause let me tell you
how our strokes paint the boardwalks in a colorless world.

Like bees that transfer pollen between flowering plants to help
them grow, to make the cycle of life flow, we were birthed and
carried, then birth and carry cycles of life glow.

One who's asked to fly with bound wings, we make do and we
glide, in a colorless world, is a colored girl.
Illuminating shadowed paths, shedding light of darkened past—
to brighten the paths for our dependents and future descendants,
we are colored girls.

No longer wearing masks covering our regal elegance and class,
remorseless with our self-regard, we find art within our flaws.
Painted with delicate paragon, with weighted crowns and
weightless nouns
we walk in color bound,
that's right, we are—colored girls.

Standing out where so many stand in, not hiding the skin we're in.
Petals of duty, yet depth of immeasurable beauty, we bathe in
splendor... found in the rose of nectar;
We are colored girls.
To the young and old, we renew lessons, pray for continued blessings.
Through tears, we divulge years of dressings, barriers we were told
to hide,
spewed untrue facts of lies, all within a colorless world.

Wisdom grows from our eyes, able to see the splendid color within
our tribe; we bear fruitful fruits, and carry legacies of pride, by

staying connected to our roots.
Displaying lineage of royalty in our bones, we walk as many and
love all and any
who water our colored girls.

Black Women

Black women,
Black women,
Black women.

Those two words curate power and movement.

To desecrate on a black woman is to desecrate on oneself.

We are history, future, present, and the establishment of wealth.
We carry the soil, the water, and the rose.
A garden is formed upon the wisdom which we hold.

Princes emulate what they see from their Kings, so Kings, be
mindful of how you treat your Queens.
Don't forget kingdoms are built to usher Queens into them.

It is ignorance when one can't respect. We get quoted liked
authors from our hair down to our threads, with no footnotes on
ledgers. However, we receive a plethora of insulting and negative
connotations and epithets.

Queens, let us begin to tackle the taboos because we analogue
issues many don't delve into.

(Like) Why haven't more addressed the disparities between black
women and the lack of quality health care management?
So many don't even know we're three to four times more likely to
experience a pregnancy-related death.
Or that our symptoms go unaddressed, even when we advocate
three times more for them to run more tests.

Or how about when our lives get taken on the streets, it gets
chalked up to
"Maybe she copped an attitude on the scene" or " she wasn't
patient enough," as if patience wasn't embedded into the fibers of
our beings.

Double standards—we're the warriors, advocates, lovers, and
friends...
Our smile holds a legacy of strength. Our features are admired,
robbed and left naked of respectful salutation attire.
We carry weight in our bones from worrying about our sons,
husbands, uncles, and brothers coming home, but never sit idle...

Black women, we: march, pray, walk, advocate, moderate talks; we
make movements to push improvements for our communities, we
look for ways to bring unity.

More need to be held accountable when black women are
mistreated, underpaid, overlooked, objectified, and abused.
(Because) we are the embodiment of culture.
Yet respect isn't fostered.

Black women,
Black women,
Black women.

Two words that curate power and movement.

Angry Black Women Paradox

We are not angry; we are tolerant, tolerant that we live by a different set of rules.

Tolerant that regardless of the hurt, the abuse, the mental inflictions that we have been subject to, we will be judged before we even enter a room.

We are not "angry black women"; we're just tired, exploited, and hurt.

Our counterparts feel they have the upper hand because they weren't blessed with these curves. While we carried the burden of the scars and wiped history's tears, we served as the backbone while the flesh made appearances.

Tired

From making the countless beds on which they comfortably rested their heads, cooking the many meals that kept their stomachs fed, shining the abundant shoes they proudly marched in; writing and revising the speeches with no acknowledgments.

Exploited?

YES! Generations of teasing, mocking, and shame objectify features we were born with (our lips, hips, and derrieres) only to profit off of and capitalize on their gains.

How so many also forget our efforts and accomplishments. Blood, sweat, and tears in progressing the status quo, yet left out of history books and stories told.

Hurt

Absolutely. The labels, the name-calling, the stares. How dare you judge a women's hand when the hand she was dealt wasn't fair?

We work harder, study longer, only to be passed by, and they can't pronounce our names so our names get cast aside.

We are not "angry black women";

We are simply women that are black; our anatomy and skin tone make up the reasons for attack.

Queen Talk

Malcolm spoke the truth in 1962. He said
"The most disrespected person for certain is the black women…"
Queens, he went on to preach that we're the most neglected beings.
Let's not lose a second; how they view us is irrelevant, but how we
view us is the question. We need to learn our lessons.

We've been afforded more opportunities to represent; a relay is
what we're in.
We need to be ready to pass on the baton, so sisters, let's be
mindful of what we wish to pass on.

Sojourner Truth, Tubman, and Parks left their mark; let's leave our
daughters with our parts, some wisdom to impart.
Lesson 1: We need to address how the moon greets the sun.
Referencing each other as "my bit**" is liable to leave a stench, and
your presence is too rich, and with such, its power is diminished.

Let's acknowledge our presence with relevance,
My queen, my empress, sister, child, love, or goddess, because you
are where my heart is.

Lesson 2: My sisters' keeper through and through.

When she's down, I should do my part, protect her heart, tell her
how she is beautiful and smart; support her dreams, develop her
ambition, tackle each benchmark with precision.

Lesson 3:
Feed her knowledge, grow with her, learn from her, that's Queen
power.

Pause

Forget politically correct, let's for once hit pause and be
unapologetic for a sec.

It's time to address what has so many of us up in arms; this is
going to be a rhyme and reason for a cause.
I just want to make clear—how many of us got to disappear before
you take it there?

Let's be honest; it's easier to steal women that look like me, because
the sad reality is that there won't be much publicity.
Are we even aware of how unaware we've come to be?

Hundreds and thousands of our queens vanishing from our
streets.

Please excuse my hesitations for our legacy, to trust in this
administration or authorities.

No longer can we sit idle and act like it's not vital that each day
we're losing precious jewels, sisters are disappearing at alarming
rates, and no one's telling us the truth.
And let's not act like it's a coincidence, the uptick in the organ
trade.
Where do you think they're getting them?

Black market still the market to trade our black bodies for a profit,
and this sex-trafficking game makes a billion dollars in profit;
that's far too much money for no one to know these culprits.

So, while tweeter-finger POTUS and reality stars' nude photos get
the focus,

black women are going extinct—no one is taking notice.

This needs to be our top priority— because mothers, sisters,
daughters, wives are vanishing from OUR communities.
Forget the fake pleasantries. It's up to you and me to conduct
search parties day and night,
tell their stories, say their names, and shine their lights.

Be vigilant anti anything against our communities—
My sister's keeper I will always be.

Let's pause for those still missing in our streets.

*"Twitter finger Potus" was in reference to the administration of
2016

Kings

Let me take a moment or two to give much respect to the brothas
that make a difference in this world.
From teachers to preachers, bank keepers, pro-leaguers, writers,
engineers, all frontiers, here we honor you.
Our fathers, brothers, husbands, and sons, each crown on your
head is a much-deserved one.
From birth all through life, you suffer plagues day and night.
Misjudged and born a target to fight.
But your strength was gifted through God's might...
And there's no equal to your hustle and resilience for our people.
Your heart, those marks, your battle; I'll be your sequel.
There to support and uplift; Bonnie to my Clyde, Queen to my
Slim.
My King, I pray for you, relay my admiration for you.
So, you know, I'm cemented in your growth.
I'll cheer you on in each benchmark of growth.
Celebrate your highs and carry you on your lows.
My King, they see you as a stereotype, but I see you as a divine
being.

Saartjie (Sarah) Baartman

Imagine this:
Being born into innocence.
Born in 1789,
unable to read or write,
sold off to slavery with no chance to fight.
Taken to England under false pretense,
makes no sense what happens to you next.

Your slave owners displayed you in a London cage; they cascaded,
prodded, and paraded.
They, removed you from any semblance of humane.
Spectacles laughed and called you strange.

They changed your name to a diminutive form; Saartjie became
Sarah Baartman but you were you no more.

Conflicted because you couldn't understand how they call your
God given form animalistic when painted with intrinsic hands.
Devils came and some paid more of a price to touch you, thought
you were an illusion when you were art in human form like the
Maya ruins.

They abided in a society that hated the very traits they tried to buy
into,
so instead of honoring, they tried to rape you of all virtue.
Some made complaints, took it to higher planes; you had your day
in court, but justice didn't remain.
Doctored documents, saying it was mutual plight, but how can
one sign a contract when they can't read or write?
They interrogated you with slave owners in the room, they
watched and intimidated your views.

41

Even sources today berate and defame, they're belligerent when calling out your name.
They write that it was free choice and that you went willingly, displaying yourself admittingly.
Ignorance can't buy wisdom, but these fools deny logic to stain your legitimacy

Which is the highest form of impunity.
How can they not empathize with the lack of civility?

They killed you at 26, they killed you at 26, THEY killed you at 26, in life and death, what an atrocity.
They didn't give you an autopsy; instead of laying you to rest, they disembodied you for more scientific tests.
Tried to link features to ascertain if we derived from creatures.
Justified the dissection as research.
With scalpels, but no scruples, they picked you apart.
Pickled your brain and genitals and placed them into jars.
Made a cast of your form, and put your skeleton on display at the
"Musée de l'Homme" until in 1974, removed due to final public uproar.

Still at home, you weren't no more.
In Paris until Mandela came in office in '94.
He petitioned to have you rest at home
There was struggle and debate,
France fought distaste,
They didn't want to cave, but in 2002, with reluctance, they gave Africa back to you.
Back home you went to be, finally resting in South Africa at peace.

Saartjie Baartman, this poem is to honor you with love, empathy, and truth.
Since they couldn't apologize here's my apology to you

Love Me

I'm strong but at times still feel weak.
I'm a multifaceted, contradictory.
Can you hold me without touching me?
Talk to me without saying a word to me?
Drink in my silence, inquire about habits, examine my passions,
make love even in my absence by climbing to my frequency?
Can we converse over equality, justice, and how to make a change
   to our community?

Exchange something far more intimate than intimacy—our fears,
   doubts, our goals, and aspirational beings?

Creating safeguards for any type of weather.
Attacking our insecurities with security, knowing I got you, and
   you got me.

If the secrets to my scars were from a personal war that I wasn't
   ready for you to explore, could you still…

Love me?

Accept me in all forms of sickness and in health, in poverty or
   wealth, would you still….

Love Me?

If I expected you to pick up on my subtle cues, hold me without
   asking you to, could you still….

Love me?

If Only

Can we tell each other the truth, if only for tonight?

Let's love while making love, if only for tonight.

Talk with our hearts and not with our minds.

Let's not continue to dress our emptiness in smiles while our souls cry out.

How about we stop to object when one tries to recite how happy we've been when all that's evident is the distance.

Would you care to know how lonely I feel, even while you sit next to me, or how I yearn to feel you even while you have your arms around me?

I'm ready to hear the part I've played, what made you retract in such a way.

I will own my part in this, for what is a boat if the boat only sinks.

Was I the wind that was too harsh? Did I not support the vision you had from the start?

Did I neglect your needs in any way; tell me the truth, if only for today.

Two in One

When they write happily ever after, do they really mean that's it?
Because I feel like I married my Prince Charming, but that's where
the fairy tale ends.
We can be in the same room yet miles and miles apart.
I can be right next to you and still have an aching for you in my
heart.
When we talk, it's quite funny...
No, it's actually quite sad, because it's like I'm talking to myself
with not much dialogue had.
I feel so disconnected, and I don't even know where to begin. You
used to be my best friend, so why can't I tell you how it's been?
We don't even kiss, and I remember nights when that was all we'd do.
We stopped talking to each other; before, you used to be the first
I'd run to.
Our conversations are one of delegation and some lies; our
exchanges are none; you stopped looking in my eyes.
I still love you deeply, so please don't get me wrong, I just find I'm
now turning into a skeptic. (Where does love belong?)
I've been hurt, and you may have been too, but when does two
become one, when the one has split into two?

Mama

It's been a long time coming. There have been traces of you in my
poetry,
but this is where the rubber meets the road. I'm left exposed, with
pages of me ready to unfold.

Truth be told, the hardest chapter of mine was the last chapter of
yours.
How does one part with a limb? As such, you meant more to me
than all of them.
I'm grateful for the time we shared. I'm not able to imagine a life
without air,
And you breathed life into me, like 80's Whitney, your love melody
was in perfect pitch.
I often reminisce.
I try to put myself in your shoes, which no doubt I couldn't fit.
You were younger than I am now when you flew 8,000 miles for a
better life for your child(s).
In a foreign country that you weren't accustomed to.
Culture shock would have been an upgraded view; you had no one
to lean on or talk to.
I was the youngest, and as I got older I began to understand the
complexities of a refugee.
The contrasting difference between the strength of a man and a
woman goes beyond physical entity and plays into mental grit.
His insecurities he bottled up in his fist; the bottle was his outlet.
Your insecurities you buried within yourself.
You loved harder to compensate for his cold traits. My eyes grew
wiser. He left me with a bitter taste.
You continued to carry on with regal elegance and grace.
Even when he passed, you paid respect and held our hands. You
never spoke ill of him. Your compassion is the compass I try to

48

live within.
God was your fortress, and you led our home with your heart,
selfless in all parts.
I saw the struggles, but your smile only doubled.
I'm humbled to say I shared space with a superhero, Mama. There
will never be an equal.

Butterflies

In the absence of presence, we shared butterflies,
Thoughts of he and me.
Hand in my hair, he made me smile,
while we walked, weakness cascaded in our knees.
Interlocked, we walked. He inhaled, I exhaled.
He gently held me.

He waited patiently to touch, to see, to feel, connection in just to be.
We assimilated in every way, and one day, he whispered ever so
softly,
"You make me feel…butterflies."
Heart in hand, he lifted me as we danced.
I drew him near, we lay, parlayed, head on his chest, he said,
"I would never trade this place"—I smiled,
Butterflies in midst we exchanged.

Cued

I listened and saw the patterns.

But my heart told my mind to ignore the language.

Making excuses as I placated absences as happenstances.

I deposited into an account that was void of any love language.

You withdrew with no thought or concern—that space between
parked and vacant.

I constantly ached for a taste of reciprocation.

I stood waiting, waiting, waiting....

Bankrupt, I stopped chasing, heart in mind's place, mind digesting
at a slow pace.

Fine lines now drawn on my face, eyes and ears cued to takes.

Dear X

Your silence no longer upsets me,
Your lack of touch I have accepted.
It's your ignorance of the two that I have most resented.

Love

It's as if there's a burning hole in your chest.
The pain so physical it leaves you in distress.
It's laying your nakedness at their feet.
Exposing your scars and fears hidden deep.
It's releasing the shame, ego, and pride time and time again,
only to be emotionally crippled by
your vulnerability, isolation, and disconnect.
Why did you chose to endure such a feeling?

Because your heart is held captive. LOVE has captured it.

Cost of Love

They say, "Love don't cost a thing," well, I think that's where the
fallacy begins.
It costs one pride, vulnerability to push their ego to the side;
Love is eyes wide open while sometimes playing blind.
It depletes your energy and time.
It's second chances, over many chances, hoping they'd get it right.
Love is a band-aid over an open wound; it's forgiveness with no
excuses.
Trusting your heart, exposing your battle marks; it's entangled in the
hope of it, afraid of most of it, but running into the arms of all of it.

"Love don't cost a thing"...Nah, love costs everything.
But what does it cost to be worthy of love?
See, that costs nothing.

He Lied

He said he loved me with his fist.
Counseled my tears with a kiss. What did I miss?
Courting me with flowers, attentive at each hour, my Prince
    Charming before marriage turned sour.

He called family a distraction, began subtracting my interactions.
So subtle at first, I was flattered, not knowing that love was
    rehearsed.

The first time I felt his cold hand was after a pleasant evening
    when I saw an old friend.
All he did was give me a hug, but I saw love's lips pursed, so like an
    alien, I shuffled my step, and put the gear in reverse.

That night, the look appeared in his eyes.
Detached. With no forewarning, he backhanded me, and instantly
    I cried.
My lips swollen, frozen in a trance on the floor, I buried my face in
    my hands.
Tried to navigate if it was a dream, and if so, how could I escape
    and be transported back into reality?
So naïve, bought into the kisses that followed, each time after—
    feeling so hollow.
So, I know...Love, is this how it goes?

A Good Man

A good man won't mind the extra pounds or age lines.

A good man will make you laugh, wipe your tears, and hold your hand.

He won't say all the words you want to hear but will be the voice of reason when your doubts appear.

He will draw you near while you're asleep, be up with you when you're sick or weak.

His promises he will keep.

He will give without asking to receive.

A good man won't lay a hand to hurt you, won't call you names. He will apologize when he's made a mistake.

He will learn your habits and accept your flaws, embrace your inhibitions and support your goals.

A great man will understand his responsibilities; his character will be evident by his loyalty.

Your significance in his life you won't have to guess; a great man is one you won't have to test.

A good man may not have the big account or fancy cars, but his character will be far greater than wealth can account for.

Release

I felt that gentle tug of release, your body, heart, and soul slowly
shifting from me.
I wasn't blind,
I choose not to see, deaf to what you attempted to whisper
repeatedly.
My ego, wanting to play hero, believed that by loving you more I
could make us equal.

Girlfriend

Daughter, sister, friend of mine,
It will take some time for you to see...
He was the test. Your testimony will be coming next.
It was not your fault.
Nothing you did or said. His insecurity he has yet to put to bed.
"You were too much?" Yes, I agree.
You were too sexy, smart, kind, and funny. He wasn't able to
    comprehend or grasp the weight of your beauty.
Don't look in the mirror and see what he wanted you to see;
Instead, take my eyes and see your reflection through me.

WHY...

Why is my voice deaf to your ears?
Why are you blind to my tears?
My fears are that these words won't reach you,
my fear is that these words won't teach you.

Goodbye

French-kissing my lips while your eyes wander past my face,
your disloyalty is so bitter that your tongue leaves a taste.
Why does my heart cling to residence while my brain evicts your presence?
Constant inner battle in which, win or lose, some part of me is the victim.
Mourning the memories that pass with time,
empty shell who I›m now kissing goodbye.

Love is….

Love is heavy; it's not always so merry, and it's many days of:
"I don't like you very much right now," but through whatever and
back, I'll be there at clutch.
It's respect and hard work; it's daily devotions, it's suppressed
emotions, it's curbing temptations, it's exposed and naked.
Love is allowing them to see stretch marks from growth that took
place. It's standing still and not changing face. Love is permitting
them to taste hidden places stowed away.
Love is showing them where you call home.
People think it's a bed of roses, as long as you know this: Thorns
are interlaced at the stem.
Love is as beautiful as it is painful, somewhat relatable to them.
But,
This I know: Love is air to the soul. It's poetry to a pen; it's stillness
in mayhem; it's choosing to step over grenades day after day,
surrendering to a war that your body craves.

Day Dreaming

I imagined I was your sun in the morning, but you cast me as your
cloud...
I imagined I was your peace in the evening, but you drowned me
out with sound.
I imagined I would be happy, but somber I have become... because
I have made you everything, and in (your) everything, I wasn't
found.

Unhinged

With gritted teeth and contrived eyes, you speak through me.
With a heart of stone and fist of steel, you puncture my soul with
each jeer.
From fallen promises to mascara tear stains, I search for the home
in your eyes, and only find pain – I've lost myself trying to find
you, too unhinged to ascertain that you've lost yourself too.

Dear John

Dear John,

I guess you've known for some time now that things haven't been
    sitting well.

I thought I'd write you this letter so I don't harbor regret.

Before I say goodbye, here are the reasons why I left:

I gave you more than I gave myself.

Into a bankrupt account, I deposited my wealth.

I would feel the warmth of our bed only to turn and catch

The emptiness and coldness of the edge.

I once counted hours in a week, then weeks in years, patiently...

when you know patient isn't me.

I tried. Spent years believing that by cultivating fruits in each
    season

somehow come harvest I might taste the nectar of juice.

That maybe it'll be my turn to feel the sun on my face,

caressing me with its arms. But you were always gone, armed with
    excuses focused on your movements.

I tried new hairdos, bought dresses with you in mind, wondering
    if you'd be pleased, only to show up and have you not even
    notice me.

Foreign and archaic I became to myself..

I wondered what I could do to have love reciprocated.

I waited but still there was no depth.

You showed me that I was last on your list.

I didn't want to believe it till I was able to see it.

Did you know it was our anniversary last week?

I went out and bought roses, put them in a vase on the front table.
You walked in, then walked by, kissed me on my cheek, and asked,
"Baby, what is there to eat?" My heart died a little that day ...
I would tell myself those things were trivial, that we would be
  okay.

But, then your disappearing acts began taking center stage.
It was at times when I needed you the most;
Do you remember when I started calling you my "Casper the
  friendly ghost"?
You laughed, but I didn't… because it was real for me, but you
  didn't get it.
You see, I told you I didn't believe in love. I tried holding back, but
  you reassured me, told me to trust—man... why did I believe
  that?
Case in point, here I am sitting writing this letter to the man to
  whom
I thought I would say my "I do's."
The hand I held, believing it was gonna be you that I would bear a
  son to.
But I guess it wasn't in the stars because, while I orbited you as my
  sun,
you were in another galaxy. Maybe this was all just a fantasy.

Signing off,
Jane

Love Capsule

Some treasure items and bury them in the ground, my capsule
found its way to me decades ago in my hometown.
With him is my youth and old age,
my what was, what is, and what will become, through God's grace.
With time there came phases, from honeymoon to damn we
doomed, to baby let's make changes.
I'm not lucky, I count myself blessed because even at our worst his
patience stood the test.
Even through unrest, we drew on the good times during our most
trying times to find inspiration in the next.
Weathering many storms through God as our foundation.
Determined to form rainbows after the rain, we turned tears into
lessons, love isn't just a word it's an action.

You (Kelelaye), are my capsule in human form, with you are my
dearest memories and my future goals.

Conscious View

My eyes have witnessed pain far greater than my ability to
rationalize the irrationalities of disparity and inequality.
My heart is heavy from conscious awakening that my limits have
limits yet limitless possibilities if constraints weren't conformed to
retain but rather engage and educate to free the mentally enslaved.

Genocide

There's a war on the streets, a genocide it would be labeled if taken place in another country.

Black men, women, and children are murdered countlessly, And all because of the color we were born to be.

Black men targeted and killed is not an "all lives matter," but a black lives matter.

It's matter and cause for us. Are there any other races being targeted but us?

Unapologetically they kill us, and unapologetically we rise.

Label it as riot when we march on the streets for peace, label us terrorists because we use our voices to speak.

The distaste in my mouth as another one is let free, protected by their shield while justice bleeds.

Strategies

Whether we wear our hoodies, walking home from the corner store,
standing on our block,
driving while black, or jogging on the spot,
we are at a loss….
how to teach our kids strategies for not getting shot...
Cause truth is, the trigger MAN is useless, drowning in his own
filth and rage,
permitted with a license to take out, and be acquitted on stage.

So, what do I teach my kids?

I teach them to love and pray...
Be diligent at observing but for certain not to let weak minds
suffocate,
for fear is not from God.
To love with intention and not use the same recipe for perception.
Never judge by the color of skin, economic or social status a
person is in.
Navigate life with no worries or mentions.
Tomorrow is not promised, so today is high fruit (Son),
(Daughter) Make sure to wear proudly your roots,
live boldly and stake claim so there is no mistake that you made a
mark, and inked your name.

I tell them to leave seeds planted so the next generation will know
that in our present day,
WE
Walked, marched, jogged, fought, died, lived, loved with heart,
and wore our skin as a badge of honor.
That we paved a way so that they may know that their existence is
relevant.

So that when they walk out their door, they can smile casually and
not be looked at as a threat
and be made a casualty.

Tuskegee Study

The Tuskegee Study of Untreated Syphilis is infamous.

Six hundred men studied like mice in a lab, 66 percent with syphilis, the others healthy yet prodded and poked, spinal taps conducted like that shit was a joke.

Even with treatment discovered, patients were left untreated and unrecovered.

Projected duration of experiment to be six months but lasted forty years.

Where's the humanity in exposing the healthy to insanity?

This was in the United States, in 1932.

The "negro" men were left blind, crippled, and abused.

All to see how untreated disease would look to be,

patients were fed a dream and $50 dollars for a burial fee.

"Bad blood" was the blanket excuse.

The men weren't told what they had or that they were being used.

Conspiracy so thick and laced with cruelty, my heart continues to break at the many casualties. The Public Health Service was in charge of this disservice.

They didn't have the dignity to lead with integrity,

Patients never consented, medical apartheid following slavery.

Not Guilty

Fist balled up, eyes dried out from tears, heart aching so bad you
swear your eardrums can hear the beatings of your fear... Mind
racing, frustration turned to anger, then rage.
Body seizes with unrest. Tell me how you would react to another
"NOT Guilty" verdict?
Weapon found? Yes.
The suspect placed on "administrative leave," paid vacation's all
that means, while they take time to assassinate the character of the
child left dead on the streets.
The man who killed your son, brother or friend walks out of the
courtroom acquitted, which in itself is a crime within a crime
committed.
Convicted or acquitted, the justice system is not designed for "us."
So too, I find comfort in knowing it's in my God I trust!
And on Judgment Day, your race, wealth, power, privilege and
shield won't help your case, and precedent will not factor in the
sentence you will face.
My justice comes from powers not found in jurors, judges, or men,
and the penalty will be far greater than a courtroom can grant.

Lights out

Peaceful we stand with tape across our lips. The Justice System
abuses us like the cops abused King*.
Asked to trust in a system that has no trust in us, they tell us to
"move on" when we're still at the back of the bus.
"You have laws," they say, the same rights as all men, yet a man
that kills a boy walking home is innocent, and the man that kills a
dog is the one that gets the charge. Tell me the system isn't flawed.
We aren't entitled to "their" laws; you can sit at the table but only
eat the crumbs that fall.
Beaten in words and stereotypes and asked to applaud, robbed of
culture and our words yet still asked to simply nod.
These are our sons that are laid to rest. These are our sons who are
marching frustrated, confused, and upset.
Broken hearts and tear-stricken eyes, yet they ignore and ask us to
sympathize.

* Rodney King and the 1991 attack.

Slavery

God created you, and he certainly created me,
yet you feel entitled to tax my life and barter for your personal
  greed.
Who gave you the right to a life outside of your own—to hold a
  gun to my head for a sense of control?
Man to man, what kind of man has to bind to beat?
What kind of man steals, buys, and trades in bodies?
I may be the one in shackles, but you are the one living in slavery,
  submitting to the demon that whispers hate and to carry out
  acts of brutality.

Monster in my closet

I knew there was something off, something in your tone and the
address and topics of our talks.
I was a child, so I shrugged these hesitations off. Plus you were
never a "stranger," so there wasn't a cause for me to feel imminent
danger.
Polite and smiling but always seemed obliging.
Always seemed more affectionate. Something within me was more
reserved and hesitant.
At the time, I couldn't reason what it meant.
My intuition was far wiser than me.
I reasoned with my conscience; I forgave the awkward silence,
the glances I was uncomfortable with, but I blamed myself for
thinking of you any less.
I was naive in true child form, but you knew this of me, and that
was what turned you on.
A predator hunts what he knows, and you took the time to know me.
Hindsight now 20/20.
All those questions, your curiosity, and some sexual suggestions,
even asking my preferences.
You were sick and I thought, "Maybe all adults think like this."
You had things we didn't; you capitalized on our humble
beginnings.
You lured me with Tetris and other materialistic ish.
You studied my family dynamics: single mother, how I loved her.
You used all of it.
She trusted you and you betrayed me.
I couldn't stab her with the truth. You knew that would break her
heart, and I wouldn't play that part, so you continued the abuse.
You volunteered to watch me. I would protest, but with no valid
address, my reluctance sounded like a tantrum at best.
Now, looking back at what you did, it all disgusts me.

F**k the physical shit—I mean the mental monopoly.
You had me sitting in jail while you moved around and bought
property.
You toured the board; you smiled so casually.
You played your role so well,
and that's the shit that bothers me.

Scale

Too much is at stake for us to look away.
Too many lives have passed on while onlookers moved on.
Seems the measure of life is weighed on a scale of complexion.
The fairer the skin the less offensive.
Seems unfair, but that's the hand we're dealt in.

Urban Planning

So much violence in the community when low income meets underserved minorities.

Interesting how the schools that need the funding are crowded with bureaucracy. Drop out statistics are in the double digits, yet news outlets won't tell you this. When the protests are on display, they label them as riots.

Freedom of speech is impeached, to silence the voices that tried to speak.

Easy to blame the youths for the problems we see. Like a magician hiding cards behind the sleeve.

Who do you think supplies the guns, pills, and weed?

Who funds alcohol stores on each block down the street?

Why is "urban planning" not challenged in our communities?

Victims become "suspects," then neglected by a society manipulated by the media into believing they were thugs, you see;

The projects were a project to contain us in modern day slavery.

Why are our youth referred to as "thugs," "gangsters," and "monsters"?

If one read between the lines, ignorance would be found in that answer.

Different skin tones will dictate the intro. Tell me our youths are
   not set up for systematic abuse.

The projects were a project to project their agenda and views.

Bravery is every man on the streets who, despite statistics, dreams
   of being that flower that grows from concrete.

Dream

It's a fallacy that their* dream wasn't one.
They both had a dream, and their dream bore a son**.
Silence is no longer the phase, no longer the victim or the prey.
People are forming protests and calling their names.
Hands up, don't shoot.
We're just trying to breathe because they both had a dream.

*Malcolm X and Martin Luther King
** Barack Obama

Hostile

Hostile takeover may as well be your slogan on TV.
With hostility and arrogance, you patrol our streets.
Who chose who as the enemy when discrimination and police
brutality are more prevalent toward minorities?
Failing to protect and serve the segment that most needed your
security.
There are some that use their blue shields as justification to rape
our ability to walk free.
Profile the black man while setting the white man free, all for the
same offense. Yet you take offense when race is the reason we suggest.
"You have hostility?" you ask. Well, quite frankly... YES!
It's because of your lack of empathy and your forms of address.
Don't come for my son, shoot my husband, incarcerate my father
and ask me to feel refuge in dialing 911.

Innocence Lost!

When is that point where a child is no more?
When is the time where they grow up faster than before?
Innocence of a world that could have been. They trusted you and
  let you in.

I was so young but still remember that time. You were a trusted
  friend.
How dare you try—
Try to act as if what happened didn't happen. I bear the scars.
Try to act as if what happened didn't happen. You scarred my heart.
Try to act as if it was okay. I was just a child when we laid.

I have a child now, and it's quite a shame; I guard anyone that says
  his name.
Fearful of those that resemble a foe, can't even trust him with
  those that I think I know.
He will not know what we know until he grows older.
For now, I just have to be strong when he doesn't understand why
  there are no sleepovers.

I grant you forgiveness and grant greater to myself.
Thought it was my fault, but I've gained so much wealth.
Wealth in understanding and wisdom. It is all so clear. It was your
  inability to deal with your tears.
You were ill-prepared and couldn't handle the pain.
From victim to villain with time you became.
I pray you find the healing you so desperately require;
I relinquish you as the monster of my past, only the reference
  point of when innocence would retract.

For, once innocence is lost, you can't get it back.

Patriotic

If protests against injustice and unrest offend you,
If kneeling to the flag to signify our solidarity to stand against
    wrongful killings and inhumane acts of race disturb you ….
Then we can conclude we don't subscribe to your "patriotic" views.

Irrational

I find myself trying to rationalize the irrational.

We know the victim and the culprit, yet

24-hour news outlets will conjure images with smidges; before
daybreak, America will be confused, assuming the victim was
responsible for being abused.

All the while I am unamused at how the "Justice System" is ill
prepreared to manage truths.

Desensitizing injustices will leave corrupt authority as the
majority.

Each life taken should not be taken so lightly.

Shedding light is how we bring light into these tragedies.

Shadows

I hear your footsteps from behind. I look; you flash an awkward
   smile.
Feeling uneasy at the center of my pit, my tempo rises, yours skips.
My heart begins to race. "Please God, no!"—but it's too late.
You shove me over and whisper, not a shout. I feel your hands
   now over my mouth, damp and sturdy, pinching my chin. I will
   never forget how I cried within.
My heart is racing—I scream *No!* Your punch felt so hollow.
We lock eyes, then I see: mine filled with horror; yours empty.
Your body so heavy, mine now frail, you engage without warning,
   my tears turn into wails.
Trying to take over all that I have within. When you finished, you
   smiled with an "I conquered" grin.
However, I left the second you arose. My body may be still, but my
   spirit roars.
Here I stand stronger than before. Here I am, you are no more, I
   will be the voice of what was and could have been. I will stand
   up and say, "NO more." You don't win. My spirit is too strong
   for you to break, my strength lies in the numbers of the ones
   you will not again take. I will stand in a courtroom with my
   head high, I will speak in rallies and in the valleys wherever
   they may lie, to an ear I will tell my story once more, to a
   classroom I will tell of your defeat and our war.

A wise man once said, hurt people hurt people, well….NO MORE.

Convicted

(When will they see us?)

Wrongfully convicted
imagine being a kid interrogated for a crime where you're the
subject of their convictions.
Press conference to denounce that "systematic racism" existed–
Well, shame on you, America, data supports what we've known;
Justice for us has consistently not been afforded.

George Stinney
14, 90 lbs.
Never an incident of ever hurting anyone.
No evidence found, no witnesses, no provocation,
no malice, no intent, no justifiable reason to commit the offense,
nonetheless, Jury of three officers sentenced him to death.

Youngest in history for capital punishment.
Victim of judicial prejudice in this case is clear,
sixty years for his name to be cleared.

Kalif Browder
Walking home from a party in Le Bronx.
He was sixteen when police picked him up.
Suspect of an attempted robbery,
how suspect, no goods found in his pockets,
But a black boy or man in America is guilty until acquitted.
Waited three years in Riker's prison, forgotten by the system.
Physically and sexually abused; this was the epitome of systemic
abuse.
Where was child advocacy when this child's rights were refused?

Justice system is a system that justly does us unright. Sixteen years old, you shouldn't have to fight for your life.
Released on wrongful imprisonment but still imprisoned in his mind.
May his soul rest eternally in peace, and may this story disturb your peace of mind.

Central Park 5

Donald Trump took up an ad to advocate for them to lose their lives.
Vowing they were telling the truth, five young boys, seven hours in an interrogation room.
But by deaf ears their pleas were ignored. Truth isn't what the authorities sought; their stories didn't align with the timeline they concocted. So, they fed them details and asked them to recant their stories.
Over and over again, mind-manipulating babies for their glory.
Imagine being a child and growing up with dreams, only for the world to paint you as a demon, knowing what they said was untrue, that the lies that were told didn't depict the real view.
Coerced confessions pay attention to a system that fails our youth with no question.

Johnny Hincappea

A Columbian from Queens, when the police picked him up him, he had just turned eighteen.
They dragged him out his house.
His mother pleaded for them to stop.
She asked if they'd need a lawyer; they lied and said they'd not.
They beat and tried to coerce him while they questioned his whereabouts.
His story never changed; some witnesses even vouched.
Wrote and told his story, begged for someone to hear, and finally,

it happened. Twenty-five years later, he was cleared.

The real culprits are these corrupt authorities who dishonor and
dismantle the truth, locking it up, then sleeping comfortably,
protected by a flawed system of abuse.

In all these cases: no DNA, no evidence, no witnesses, no intent,
no malice, no provocation.
Just people in power with prejudice.

Wild Thoughts

Seems every time the news is on, it's only speaking of tragedies.
Anxiety so high, I sometimes doubt my own sanity.
Frustrated, dismayed, and angry at the irony, the "killed my
    brother so your brother must die" mentality.
Ignorance and hate weigh heavy on our societies.
Virtual reality, the escape, is now our sad reality.
If humanity was valued as a commodity, how many of us would
    use it as currency?
Would we value it more than diamonds and gold and begin to
    treat it as a priority?
If conversation negated wars and dialogue was carried forth with
    honesty, could we look past our pride to bring our ancestors
    dreams of equality?
Working together beyond creed, origin, and nationality, with
    courage and unity for the common goal of peace.
If we each shared our bread, wouldn't everyone have something to
    eat?

Strength

Strength doesn't come from beating your chest.
It's not about the weights or the quantity of reps.
It's not about an athlete's size or build,
not how many quarrels were won nor weapons fueled.
Strength is not dressed in pants or skirt.
Age is not a hindrance, and wealth cannot buy into it.
Strength is born when one endures.
When, paralyzed by fear, perseverance answers the door.
When tears are wiped to continue the fight, win or lose,
strength is confronting the enemy at sight.
Scared or weak, strength is standing on your feet.
Strength is humility in the presence (or absence) of success.
It's smiling when you're crying inside.
It's forgoing ego and pride.
Strength is gained from lessons of pain.
Standing tall despite the many falls.
Weakness is Strength camouflaged.

Fallen

Fallen down more times than I can count.
Countless times that I've counted myself out.
Lord forgive me, but if you can only shout,
see I'm trying to listen but my doubts drown your sound.

It's like a whisper, and I'm trying to quiet down;
my sin lingers, everything around me is so loud.

I guess I'm trying to find my footing in your will.
Trying to discern if I'm superimposing in it still.
This world is falling and it's trying to pull me in its descent.
My soul is parting and it's feeling so intense.

Help me, Lord, please take my weakness in your strength
I'm a sinner who's falling but I'm reaching for your hands.

Normalcy

Fragments of you still live when you do inordinate things like….
Sing and dance in the middle of an aisle
Or
smile at a stranger just for walking by you.
Unguarded, but only for a fraction until the reactions of this world
reinforce that joy is a distraction.
I'd tell you to stop listening, to cover your ears; those that have
fears believe in a cocktail of misery in company.
But that isn't the company you need to keep—normalcy is only for
the weak.

Nola

Daughter of mine, I hope you take with you this:
You can be anything you wish.
I've been captivated ever since our first engagement.
Recoil at time that's so elusive, you've transformed before my eyes,
little girl to young lady in one swift movement.
Shy before, now fearless you've grown to be, intelligent, beautiful,
and wise.
How your ways inspire and amaze me.
You will blaze the trails; there are no doubts or maybes.
A force to be reckoned with, but always my baby.

You (Mikael)

Raw emotions set in motion from the moment of your first cry.
Perfect love was set in cement; you are the human form of my
heart in existence.
When I want to see God's majesty, I take a look at you; God's
intrinsic work is really quite a view.
For the rest of my life, I have the joy and responsibility of raising
you; every heartache for you will be one for me, too. Sweet,
precious one, don't lose sight of this,
Words won't contain the deep connection that exists.
Our oneness has taken on two forms, but you are an extension of
an extension that will extend into generations not yet born.
I see the greatest version of who I want to be, and the earliest
adaptation of who I tried to be all wrapped up in who you're
growing to be, and I give thanks each day.
The birth of you was the birth of me; you are love personified to an
infinite degree.

Reminisce

Reminisce on the days of hopscotch, double dutch, and listening
to mixtapes.
Eating patty and coco bread while sipping on Kool-Aid.
80's gal, but the 90's raised me;
227, Cosby, Martin, and *Living Single* on TV.
Melodies of Jodeci and SWV get me "weak in the knees," so much
so that
I could hardly breathe.
Bliss was watching the boys play hoops in Fila kicks, giggling with
my homegirl while whispering secrets of who we would want to
kiss….
Remember this?
How I often reminisce.

Life

Why do we wait for the day when one passes to celebrate and
    reflect
on their life and the legacy it impacted?
Flowers after hours, whom can delight?
For loving while living is what we need to strive toward.
Eulogize, compliment, express heartfelt sentiments;
life may be shorter than you expect.
Pour champagne while you can make a toast of life's evidence.
in life, let's pay tribute to the living who can absorb it.
Paying tribute is the last act of love we are afforded.

What if?

What if you knew she saw you?
Saw the anger, the rage, the prejudice you put her family through.
Would the rivers of tears make it clear that her pain is real?
If you can sense her leaves tremored fear, would you lay your
    bitterness to rest?
Can your pride make way to conversing over delicate subjects?
Like the root of hate being fear, inferiority complex creates the
    disillusionment that there is an us and you, and the us is the
    anthesis of good, robbed of virtue to massage your conscience
    when carrying out acts of unconscionable cruelty .
Would you hold her hand to explain how one God can favor either
    the sun or the rain?
Impossible… (yes?) since both were created for divine purposes.
Then how can one man assume that a merciful God would
    condone hate against anyone that He created His own?

Poem Inspired by the art of Komla Letsu Philip

Black Girl Magic

Her smile alludes to what it is…
She has fire in her spirit.
Strength is kin, adversities she wins by displaying them as a badge
of honor.
Inherited resilience that was a gift from her ancestors.
Creativity like a limb you confuse for hidden powers.
Her backbone is her faith; there's no mistaking her character.
Integrity is the cloak she wears, yet mystery surrounds her.
When walking into a room, she observes the wolves who gather
In sheep's clothing; she is tuned to read and discern the lines
between the chatter.
Her intelligence is evident, streetwise and on the corporate ladder.
She has depths running from her locs to her toes; beauty is upon
her.
A chameleon that can move smooth as jazz, from high heels
to marching boots.
From power points, to protesting on civil rights movements.
Her elegance lies in her humbleness.
She embodies… Black Girl Magic.

Escape

Give me an escape, if only for a moment.
Take me past the sum of my reality to a place where I can forget
the weight of my liabilities, enjoy the treasures life has for me
without worry or care of life's complexities.

Growth

In between the spaces (<>) lies growth.
My mind traces the evolution of choices, both good and bad,
that have sustained me.
To stand planted in the consciousness of where and who I am.
Never complicated, yet underrated,
I'm the flying spirit of one who is free.
In between the spaces lies who I was and who I'm trying to be.

LIVE

If life is what you make it, then why can't many make it?
Passion is left idle for peace of mind,
for fear of living has robbed so many blind.

Society teaches us to trade our happiness for a false sense of success,
Securing a 9 to 5 while relinquishing our childhood dreams,
believing that's what's best.
Living while not living, so many retiring on life.

Ever stop to ask why and where do I fit in?
Then again, who has the time? Read blogs to develop a frame of
mind.
No time to question whether the life you're living is it, so you cut
pieces of the puzzle to make it fit.
But one can't lose sight of this—during the final moments of life,
can we really say we lived?

Immigration

If the borders kept you out, you wouldn't be let in.
Think about your ancestors and where it really began.

Human decency is a decency;
separating kids is an atrocity.
We all migrated into this free nation.
You have babies who had no choice now sleeping on pavements.

Where is the sense of urgency,
what's the crime in diplomacy?
Where did your heart go? You voted in one with a monstrous ego
who views blacks as Negros, Latin brothers as thieves,
and Muslims as lethal when God called us all equal.

1900 kids and women in South Texas confined to what I call a
prison,
is this "Making America Great Again"?
Tell me what I'm missing. Are three-year-old kids a threat?
Then why do they have guards outside their rooms and keep them
detached from their beds?
If this happened to you, you'd be calling the feds.
I'd get an alert on my phone.
Just cause their name is not "Amber" doesn't mean the government
should lower the standards.
Dividing people into White or others that are not right is page
from Hitler.
WE, need to wake up!

If not you, then who?
If not me, then WE;
Must raise up, protect each other, as brothers and sisters; look

past skin, creed, and religion.
Wrong is wrong, regardless of which political side you're on.
This is not about rhymes, it's about the moral crimes that won't
stop
till we start rising up and saying, "Your time is up!"

Role Models

When did baring all become the platform for feminist
    empowerment?
How are the women who pose nude now the role models for
    success?
Why are augmented bodies, those that filter their lives for hobby,
    admired?
We hold viewership and follows as a map to navigate and aspire to.
Women showing more than less.
Promiscuity accepted as the standard, and virtues put to the test.
We used to fight for equality and respect.
How sad the shift and distorted views.
Misguided society that feeds into insecure movements.
If we are not careful, our young girls will buy into this tragedy;
Blind leading the blind, with no sense of dignity or morality.

Question

What if each person took the initiative to enrich another person's
life?
If we were our brothers' keepers and dug deeper,
being mindful that our roles of mentor or teacher could be ones
that feed
A generation or nation, would you then pay attention?
What if the currency for life's lessons was humbleness,
And we each shared our trials and tribulations to success—
would that hurt or help your sister in distress?
If we valued conversation over scripted reality TV;
If social media took a back seat to reality.
Would our interpersonal connection grow to be strong or weak?
What if equality was accepted, size, color, origin, and creed was
respected? Would there be strife or cause for war?
Just a question.

Survival apparatus

I smile so hard my stomach hurts when I think about myself.

See, out of clenched bars of hurt, I escaped seemingly safe and sound.

Teetering fragility is tucked inside a hardened shell.

My greetings and surface pleasantries I find can be Oscar-bound.

I prance around in normalcy when stirring in self-doubt.

Many often look at me and assume they see what I'm about.

What is offered to view is often reviewed and modified for the discretion of the viewers...

So, don't buy what one lays down when it could be filtered maneuvers.

When I think about myself, I smile, for it's an extension of a frown.

A smile is a far more dangerous apparatus than then a higher octave sound.

Inspired by my forever poet muse Maya Angelou and one of my favorite poems "The Mask."

Bathe

I bathed myself in insecurities.
Lathered myself in self-doubt.
I sulked in water,
I let my head dip back.
My muscles relaxed
In waters unclean
I accepted lies as facts.
Stained mirror glass,
Strained reflection back,
I take a picture as evidence
So the shadows can retract

Reflections

I forgave me...then I trespassed, got drunk on past mishaps, delved
into familiar transgressions.

I thought I had learned my lessons; I thought I wouldn't relive this
present.
I thought burying it meant I deaded it, but instead, I carried it.
I somehow must have treasured it, because the pain was intact,
perfectly wrapped.
I could no longer run from my past,
I could no longer put on a mask; I sat in it...

Entangling the layers, I kept hiding, and at one point, I felt like
I was drowning; I felt myself gasping for air. The silence was
deafening to my ears.
I then exhaled, I'm through playing musical chairs,
I claim this seat right here.
I claim my happiness.
I'm too grown to care what anyone else thinks.
I've lived, but only in context.
I'm ready to hear what I think.
I'm welcoming my inner voice back,
I almost forgot how to do that.
I played nice,
I thought it was right to be gracious, putting their needs above my
needs, but I lost track of what I needed.
I lost track of who I was and where I was being led.
I lost track, and now... I'm tracking it back,
I'm putting it back intact. I can't recover my past, its history.
The present is all the present that I need to carve out and leave my
legacy.
The story I want told when I'm seasoned and old, ready for my

final breath to go home:
I want to say
"I lived"—and in far more than just a literal context.

Captured

Was I smiling or was I crying? was the question posed.
Fixated on the lens, my eyes tell stories untold.
There was a party all around me but I felt comfort standing to the
side.
I preferred to observe the chatter
Inner struggle abide.
I clenched the glass bottle and felt some relief.
I looked at those who were dancing and oh boy, it looked free.
Some girls whispered loudly… knew they were talking about me.
My dress was pretty tattered
I peeked down to see.
My shoes didn't help the matter
So I simply ignored,
pretended I didn't hear them when they said I was poor.
It really didn't bother me; I've heard it before
I obliged this distraction, wished it could last a bit more.
The host announced the cake was cutting and all the children were
gay.
So excited, some pushed past me
In a scurried haze.
I felt a cease in my stomach, knew the end was drawing near.
Clenched my coke ever tighter from a festering fear.
Wasn't ready to go home; I knew of the trouble that awaited.
Shook my head when an elder offered me a cake on a plate.
As the party was coming to an end, so was
my effervescent relief.
Noticed camera was about to capture, lens was focused on me.
Time stood still, as did I as I inhaled that last sip goodbye.
Solitary tear escaped from my eye.

Image by Atanur Memis

Sometimes

Sometimes I feel so lonely, I fear no one hears my cries.
Sometimes I feel so empty only a shadow resides.
My tears have taken residence on my round and plump face. Like
summer rain, they softly appear, and with harsh silence they invade.

Allusion

Her smile hides the inner struggles hidden deep.

She hurts but finds guilt in feeling weak.

Her teeth contrive as her mouth forms lies while the eyes tell the
tales of angst plagued inside.

Echo

My soul cries out in agony, not knowing what to do.
Ask God to save me from myself because self be quick to feud.
Self-sabotage in camouflage, leaving me confused.

Such opposition from within; is self-rooting to win or lose?

Catch treason with each height I climb, then fall victim to these
    heights.
Self-pestering in my ear: "You're unworthy of these flights."

What's a writer with no words to write?
A singer with a voiceless tune?
My insecurity holds potential captive in a room.

The mark between reality and dreams
I place on a weighted scale.
In life, you have the choice between playing
the lion or gazelle.

Procrastination enters matrix when on the brisk of greatness;
Mental strength is conquered when dealing with self-ailments.

Riddle Me

I'm more accustomed to magnifying my weaknesses
than priding myself on my strengths.
I digest critiques and rerun lines of defeat.
I can recall my first insult easier than my last compliment.
My biggest enemy wakes up each day to occupy my mind and
    taunt me...
it whispers limitations and confined boundaries.
Who am I?

Insecurity.

Alive

In pockets of small, few and in between,
I felt the sensation of being alive,
but moments faded faster than a dream.

What does it all mean?
That now complacency be the form of currency.
Where 9 to 5 careers are sold as forms of security.
Trading in aspirations for mortgage payments.
Ambition now lying in cul-de-sac pavements.

Is it living when one stops taking risks?
No longer free to roam without the hindrance of fearing to trip?
We all have 24 hours in a day,
but how many of us spend our time
to read, laugh, dance, and pray?

If alive means the measurement of a pulse,
it makes sense that so many roam around aimless and lost.

I write for…

I write for you: those of you who are neglected and abused.
Those that can't communicate the struggles you've been through.
I write for him, the one with balled fist and tears within.
Oppressed, depressed, and frustrated by the anger and unrest that
lies within his soul and consciousness.
I write to speak about the bullies on Wall Street and the faceless,
nameless haters on social media that spew hate from lack of
knowledge, who'd
Rather upload ignorance and inflict shame.
I write for her, she that stands in a room alone, screaming, crying
to deaf ears with stories that need to be told.
I write for me. I hear his cries, feel her pain, read the lies, and
process it all to formulate these words written for you…. The real
one I write to.

Purpose

There was a rumbling in my belly, an aching in my heart, a stirring
in my spirit, and restlessness in my thoughts.
"Purpose" I searched for, but it was hiding in the dark.
I inquired and bartered, spent hours and years trying to withstand
in wasteful careers.
All the while, how my God must have laughed, for the purpose I
was searching for was the pen that never left my hand.

Self

Self doesn't like being halo.
Self don't know self, yet self-acts like it knows.
From shells of emptiness, it carries a heavy load.
The weight of loneliness that no one quite knows.
Draped in darkness where light once glowed.

If someone ever listened, would they hear the deep woes?
Would they read the pages I lace with phonetic codes?
I blow a whisper, hoping an echo will catch its tone.
Trying to be selfless in a world where only selfishness grows.
Weeds stifle the potential and often grasp hold.
Why close eyes when the world's lies are served cold?
Mimic happiness while walking sadly alone.
I often hesitant to disclose, is there even relevance in sharing one's
    load.

Super Soul Sunday

You take pictures when you're happy, but what happens when
    you're sad?
Photographic memory outlasts Polaroids gone bad.

Many seek happiness; they want the lessons without the pain as if
    scripture hasn't forewarned us that life is not a game.

Before David and Goliath, remember, there was faith.
Before Isaac was conceived, there was a promise that God made.

Happiness is not a destination; it's a journey that we take.
Acceptance of the good and bad, the decisions that we make.
Life is a marathon; we all run the race.
When faced with some turbulence, one has to kick in faith!

Jeremiah 29:11 "Plans to prosper not to harm,"
From birth to dissension, the author had intentions all along.

John 16 reads "There will be trouble but not to be alarmed."

Horoscopes are like forecasts, they are assumptions; don't be
    charmed.

Google, Siri, and Alexa won't have the answers to this world.
The Bible is the living, breathing dictionary that can heal and bless
    the sick, wounded, and lost boy or girl.

No test without a testimony and no rainbow before the rain.
I will not forsake you is a promise that God made.
This life will often test you—no condemnation in the saved.

Potential

I see potential in me; the ambition in me won't let me sit still with
    complacency.
Words draw near to me. Those uncaptured sail away in a sea of
    forgetfulness.
Although it's left me on occasion with regret.
I do not get upset now; I'm more aware, conscious, and diligent.
It's gifted me with the ability to anchor in the greats.
Like one capturing a sunset, I've honed in to the keystrokes of
    parables.

Heavy

I will not change, though your cast of hate weighs heavy.
With each lie, infliction, and pain, we will rise despite your
  attempts to bury.
Draped in cloaks of many shades of sun-kissed melanated skin
  that with pride we will carry.
Knowledge equipped with wisdom and prayers to pass down to
  many.
We will not stop climbing or sharing our stories.
We will not hide our faces or whisper our glory.
Your anger will not simmer our desires to be.
Many lies have been told, but truth upholds and sets us free.
Your attempt at killing has only cemented the names;
Though their spirits ascended, eternal their lives became.
Unified as one, though we stand as many
Black Pride,
Black love,
Black unity.

HerPoeticTruth

Quotes

Legacy

My Legacy: May it be one you carry proudly. My name: may it be
one you say with distinction and clarity.

Growth

If I can't grow with you, I've outgrown you.

Self-Sabotage

Save me from me.
The me that tries to destroy SHE—
The she that lives within me, who I no longer see.

Riddled 2

What is ambition without execution?

Failure.

Clear

Sometimes… all it takes is a car ride and
good music to help navigate your thoughts.

Smile

In the absence of words, poetry can also be found in your smile.

Black History

We live between the history you teach,
and the stories you don't tell.

Time

Life is long enough to realize how short it is.

Conformity

Never measure your worth against your neighbors'.
Your measure of self should not be compared to a stranger.
Don't follow the trends when you can stand out as an individual as
God intended.
Why follow the norm when you were created and molded to be set
apart, no carbon copy on God's part. Even twins can be told apart.

Collectable

I pick up trinkets as I go.
Like lessons Mama left.
Trading pride and ego for slow temperament.
Looking both ways before you cross;
Light words but heavy thoughts,
Like making a decision, choosing logic over heart.

Sexy is:

Sexy is measuring your worth by your own standards, and not
allowing anyone else to define who you are.

Bravery is:

Being brave is not the lack of fear; being brave is
taking another step forward despite fear.

Sadness is:

Sadness is often derived from the detachment
of what was… or the lack of what is.

Truth is:

Truth is the irrefutable facts known to oneself; authenticity is the
conscious choice one makes to move in boldness and assurance by
one's own uninhibited truth.

Blind

If color is all you see, then you're blind.

Fear

She ever-so-delicately tiptoes around life,
as not to disturb her fears.

Myth

Impossibility is a myth one sells itself to stop
from striving toward one's excellence.

Compliance

Compliance kills potential for greatness.

Adept

In a world so cold and a life so short, it's best to conclude my worth won't be determined by 200,000 "likes" or just two, how many friend requests or Snapchat views. Socially adept to understand superficiality will breed more curiosity than Her Poetic Truth.

About the author

(HerPoeticTruth) Tarikua Emiru is a writer and poet. Born in Addis Ababa, Ethiopia, she was three years of age when she and her family immigrated to Toronto, Canada. Raised by a supportive single mother who fostered her love for film and storytelling, Tarikua began writing at a very early age; however, it wasn't until she was 11 years old and heard for the first time the work of Maya Angelou that she was captivated by the art of words and poetry. HerPoeticTruth work touches on racial, social, economic gaps, as well as culture, awareness, and love.

Currently, she resides in Northern California with her loving husband and two beautiful kids.

Tarikua (Ta-ree- qwa) in Amharic means "Her Story". People interchangeably refer to her under the translated version of her name- Herstory.

🅞 Herpoetictruth

Tarikua pictured with her family; Husband Kelelaye, children Mikael and Nola